CAMPFIRE
PRAYERS

NATE JOHNSTON

CAMPFIRE PRAYERS

A GUIDED JOURNAL FOR DISCOVERING YOUR PURPOSE

DESTINY IMAGE® PUBLISHERS, INC.
P.O. Box 310, Shippensburg, PA 17257-0310
"Promoting Inspired Lives."

This book and all other Destiny Image and Destiny Image Fiction books are available at Christian bookstores and distributors worldwide.

For more information on foreign distributors, call 717-532-3040.

Reach us on the Internet: www.destinyimage.com.

ISBN 13 TP: 978-0-7684-6367-5

For Worldwide Distribution, Printed in the U.S.A.

1 2 3 4 5 6 7 8 / 26 25 24 23 22

CONTENTS

INTRODUCTION

In a desperate season of my life when I struggled with the pain and wounds of the past, the rejection and loneliness of the present, and the pull of the Impossible calling on my life, I found myself on a road I didn't expect. It was a path that veered away from the hustle and bustle of the Christian norms I was used to and led me to the simplicity of talking to God as a Friend in a way I hadn't in a long time.

It was in this wilderness season, my pilgrimage, and my trek through unknown terrain when I began to navigate my unusual calling and found myself simply talking to the Father around the campfire.

This journal is the wilderness guide I wish I had years ago, but now it's yours. These prayers and prompts are no longer my journey but are now yours to discover and find what your heart longs for and what your Holy Spirit is leading you to find.

It's the conversation every wild-hearted lover of Jesus needs but what the busyness of life squashes and religion makes us too busy for. This journal is your guide out of the rut and back into intimate relationship with your Creator again.

Wild ones, the adventure awaits.

CHAPTER 1

FIRE IN MY BELLY

Dear Father, You created me with a fire in my belly that cannot be contained. I can't explain it away, suppress it, or hide it any longer. Instead, I give it room to begin to develop into a full flame in my life. Lord, where I have been tamed, I ask that You would unbridle me again and lead me onto the path ordained for my life, in Jesus' name.

The fire in my belly feels and looks like:

_____

_____

_____

_____

_____

_____

_____

_____

How have I or others tried to suppress, hide, or tame the fire?

_____

_____

_____

_____

_____

_____

_____

_____

How can I cooperate with God to fan my life into a roaring bonfire?

_____

_____

_____

_____

_____

_____

_____

_____

When my life is in full flame for God, it will change me and the world around me in these ways:

_____

_____

_____

_____

_____

_____

_____

_____

_____

_____

_____

_____

_____

_____

_____

_____

_____

Draw a bonfire and label each of the flames with a passion or unique expression you carry.

CHAPTER 2

A UNIQUE CALL

Father, I am beginning to see the fullness of my design and believe that I have been created perfectly and with a unique call that, while often misunderstood, has a powerful purpose in this era. Today, I shake off the many misconceptions people have of me and even I have had about myself. I embrace the true me who marches to the beat of a different drum as You have created me to do, in Jesus' name!

List three ways you can bounce back when you feel misunderstood:

_____

_____

_____

_____

_____

_____

_____

When I follow through to the next level of my perfectly unique design, it means people will see _____ _____ about me.

The misconception that people have of me that bothers me most is:

_____

_____

_____

_____

_____

_____

_____

_____

_____

_____

_____

_____

_____

_____

_____

_____

_____

The misconception that I have of myself that bothers me most is:

_____

_____

_____

_____

_____

_____

_____

Three characteristics about me that definitely march to a different drum are:

_____

_____

_____

_____

_____

_____

_____

Draw your "different drum" here, highlighting the quirky things about yourself that often people don't quite understand but are how God has created you.

CHAPTER 3

FIRST LOVE

Dear Father, help me continue in this calling in the same purity and conviction I started with and not slowly suffocate by the seductive taming of religion. Keep my passion raw and my hunger uncontainable. I want to stay wildly in love with You. If I have lost it, I ask for it back. Just keep my heart tethered to You and nothing and no one else, in Jesus' name!

Have I have been tamed by religion (man's version of God)? In what ways?

_____

_____

_____

_____

_____

_____

_____

If I have lost my grip on my first love I will grab hold of
His hand again by:

_____

_____

_____

_____

_____

_____

_____

_____

_____

_____

_____

_____

_____

_____

_____

_____

_____

_____

_____

How can you keep your heart tethered to the Lord and no one else? Write a prayer requesting His help:

_____

_____

_____

_____

_____

_____

_____

_____

_____

_____

_____

_____

_____

_____

_____

_____

_____

_____

Write a reply to yourself from the Father below. How would you want Him to answer your request?

_____

_____

_____

_____

_____

_____

_____

_____

_____

_____

_____

_____

_____

_____

_____

_____

_____

_____

_____

_____

_____

CHAPTER 4

A NEW SURRENDER

Dear Father, I surrender to Your plans for my life. I am done with feeling inactive or not living completely to the full extent of my calling; so today I ask You to visit me and ambush me. Today I stop wrestling and fighting what You have called me to and ask You to reignite my heart and shower me with fresh joy to run with it, in Jesus' name!

Whose hands are grasping the steering wheel of your life?

_____

_____

_____

_____

I'm afraid to surrender my whole life to my heavenly Father, and this is why:

_____

_____

_____

_____

_____

_____

_____

_____

How can you learn to trust Him if, deep down inside, you really don't trust Him?

_____

_____

_____

_____

_____

_____

_____

_____

Will you commit to say *yes* the next time the Lord prompts you?

_____

_____

_____

_____

_____

_____

_____

What do you need to let go of today to surrender completely?

_____

_____

_____

_____

_____

_____

_____

Draw a box below and label all the things you are surrendering to Jesus today.

CHAPTER 5

THE HABITATION

Dear Father, I give my life for Your glory, and as a worshiper at Your throne. I pray like Moses, "If Your Presence does not go with us, do not send us up from here" (Exodus 33:15). I must know Your presence and Your glory, so today I pray, "Make my life a habitation of Your presence," in Jesus' name.

Can you remember the first time you were aware of His presence? Write that experience here:

_____

_____

_____

_____

_____

_____

_____

_____

Picture yourself worshiping God at His throne. His expression as He looks at you is:

_____

_____

_____

_____

_____

_____

_____

_____

_____

_____

_____

_____

_____

_____

Knowing that I will ultimately crash and burn without His daily presence, I commit to _____ _____ each day.

My Lord's presence and glory in my life changes how I:

_____
_____
_____
_____
_____
_____
_____
_____
_____
_____
_____
_____
_____
_____
_____
_____
_____
_____
_____
_____
_____
_____
_____
_____
_____

Do you long to encounter God? Why is this important to you?

_____

_____

_____

_____

_____

_____

_____

_____

_____

_____

_____

_____

_____

_____

_____

_____

_____

_____

_____

_____

CHAPTER 6

COME AWAY WITH ME

Lord, if it's You, I want it. Prepare me for what is ahead and protect me in the secret place of the Most High (Psalm 91). I say yes to the come-away season and the call of the wild You are leading me into, wherever it takes me, in Jesus' name!

"Empty is the setup for upgrade"—**agree** or **disagree** and why?

_____

_____

_____

_____

_____

_____

_____

_____

_____

I know the Lord has prepared me and protected me so I can:

_____

_____

_____

_____

_____

_____

_____

Saying yes to the come-away season and the call of the wild means that I will:

_____

_____

_____

_____

_____

_____

_____

Saying yes to the come-away season and the call of the wild means that I won't get distracted with:

_____

_____

_____

_____

_____

_____

_____

What do I need to take my hands off of so God can have room to do what He needs to do?

_____

_____

_____

_____

_____

_____

_____

Read Psalm 91 and write your favorite verse. Why does this resonate with you?

_____

_____

_____

_____

_____

_____

_____

_____

_____

_____

_____

_____

_____

_____

_____

_____

_____

_____

_____

_____

CHAPTER 7

THE UNKNOWN ROAD

Okay, Lord, that thing inside me—that wild calling I have been ignoring—do what You want. I take my hands off, and I let go of all my man-made ideals and reputation, and I am all in for this road. I won't look back anymore, wondering what could have been, feeling shame or the words of disapproval from others. I won't fear this new road, and I won't dread the unknown anymore. Instead, I'll be a kid again, I'll live in wonder, and I'll do this because You are with me in this. You called me from my comforts and my apathy, and You didn't have to, but now I give my life to the call of the wild, in Jesus' name.

Are you willing to forfeit man's ways to follow God's ways? What would you need to forfeit?

_____

_____

_____

_____

_____

Being "a kid again" in this new context means I will:

_____

_____

_____

_____

_____

_____

_____

The fear and dread that held me back is gone because I:

_____

_____

_____

_____

_____

_____

_____

Write a rebuttal to use on the enemy the next time he lies to you about your past failures:

_____

_____

_____

_____

_____

_____

_____

Don't forget to use it! Stick it on your fridge or on the mirror where you can see it often.

CHAPTER 8

SPIRITUAL SENSES

This is a prayer of activation to ask the Lord to open up our eyes, to open up our spiritual ears, to sharpen and activate our spiritual senses in this season:

Put your hands on your eyes.

Lord, anoint my eyes so I can see. I don't just want to see in the natural, so activate my spiritual eyes to see what is taking place in the realm of the spirit and where You are taking me. Lord, help me discern, perceive, and understand this season better, in Jesus' name.

Which of your spiritual senses do you feel like you use the most?

_____

_____

_____

_____

_____

_____

Have you ever written off something your spiritual senses were showing you that you thought was just yourself?

_____

_____

_____

_____

_____

_____

_____

A time when I felt like I had good discernment was:

_____

_____

_____

_____

_____

_____

_____

Read Hebrews 5:14 and write down the right answer.
Exercising your spiritual senses helps you know:

a. What is okay to do:

_____

_____

_____

_____

b. What is not good:

_____

_____

_____

_____

c. What is good and what is evil:

_____

_____

_____

_____

_____

Write a prayer in your own words asking the Lord for an increase of your spiritual senses:

_____

_____

_____

_____

_____

_____

_____

_____

_____

_____

_____

_____

_____

_____

_____

_____

_____

_____

CHAPTER 9

NEW WINE

In the words of Brooke Fraser's song, "New Wine," pray with me, "Lord, make me a vessel, make me an offering, make me whatever You want me to be. I came here with nothing but all You have given me. Jesus, bring new wine out of me. In Your name I pray."

Q. What did the grape say when he got stepped on?

A. Nothing, he just let out a little whine. (That's a little grape humor for you at no extra cost.)

Step one of becoming fine wine is to be crushed. Are you willing to keep signing up? Can you point to a time in the past when you were crushed, pummeled, or pounded but the end result was growth?

_____

_____

_____

_____

_____

Step two to produce fine wine is the aging, waiting process. How can you chill when you feel like you're ready to go, but the Lord is saying "slow down"?

_____

_____

_____

_____

_____

_____

_____

Often when we sip the Holy Spirit's new wine we can look foolish or even rebellious. List a time you felt misunderstood when you were doing your best to follow the Lord.

_____

_____

_____

_____

_____

_____

_____

New wine is frequently misunderstood. What do you think the fruit will be of following God on this unique path?

_____

_____

_____

_____

_____

_____

_____

_____

_____

_____

_____

_____

_____

_____

_____

_____

_____

_____

_____

_____

Write or draw the fruit below.

CHAPTER 10

UNSHACKLED VOICES

Lord, You have given me a voice for a reason, and I can look back and see the many times I let others and myself shut it down out of not knowing how to use it or out of fear. Today, help me begin to see the kind of voice You have called me to be. Help me own it and steward it well, in Jesus' name.

Does your voice/gifting seem more like a curse or a blessing?

_____

_____

If you have renounced or cursed your voice or gifting, write a prayer of repentance:

_____

_____

_____

_____

What is the reason or the purpose for which God gave you a voice?

_____

_____

_____

_____

_____

_____

_____

How can you use and steward the gift that God has given you?

_____

_____

_____

_____

_____

_____

_____

What kind of voice do you want to be?

A voice of justice?

A voice of deliverance?

A voice of healing?

I want to be a voice of.........

_____

_____

_____

_____

_____

_____

_____

_____

_____

_____

_____

_____

_____

_____

_____

CHAPTER 11

THE PIONEER PATH

Lord, help me know how to pioneer well. So much is unknown, and I'm still trying to find my footing. I know that, if I keep my eyes on You, Jesus, I will run my race well and break through any hard ground before me. I'm following You, Lord, in Jesus' name.

Write Ephesians 6:16 here:

_____

_____

_____

_____

_____

_____

_____

_____

Pioneers are the ones out in front. They frequently have to dodge arrows as they plod across the barren wastelands of their journey. Which of the enemy's fiery darts have you experienced?

_____

_____

_____

_____

_____

_____

_____

_____

_____

_____

_____

_____

_____

_____

_____

_____

_____

_____

_____

Draw some arrows here and label them:

What do you need to do now to make sure you finish your future race well?

_____

_____

_____

_____

_____

_____

_____

_____

Listen to Rick Pino's song "Pioneer" on repeat!

What lyrics spoke to you?

_____

_____

_____

_____

_____

_____

_____

CHAPTER 12

GIANT SLAYERS

Lord, today I lean into You and Your ability to use me in ways beyond my capabilities. Help me discover how You have uniquely created me for this moment and activate everything that has been inside me that You want to use to take down giants and set captives free, in Jesus' name!

What unusual tools has God put inside you that when matured will make you a giant slayer?

_____

_____

_____

_____

_____

_____

_____

_____

How will you remind yourself that it's God's strength working through you and not your strength that wins the battle?

_____

_____

_____

_____

_____

_____

_____

_____

_____

_____

_____

_____

_____

_____

_____

_____

_____

_____

_____

_____

_____

Write 1 Corinthians 1:26-31:

_____

_____

_____

_____

_____

_____

_____

_____

_____

_____

_____

_____

_____

_____

_____

_____

_____

_____

Meditate on it. Memorize verse 27 and make it your life's scripture!

Draw some of your unique tools below that God has given you.

CHAPTER 13

BIRTHING SEASON

Lord, show me what I am carrying and about to birth. Show me what You have been weaving together behind the scenes that I cannot always see and bring it to fruition in my life, in Jesus' name!

The next time you feel barren, how will you battle that lie? (Hint: Isaiah 66:9.)

_____

_____

_____

_____

_____

_____

_____

_____

_____

Ask God to show you signs of life that are stirring that you may have overlooked. Write down what He says:

_____

_____

_____

_____

_____

_____

_____

_____

_____

_____

_____

_____

_____

_____

_____

_____

_____

_____

_____

During a birthing season God may begin to awaken forgotten dreams and desires. Ask God to remind you today what you have forgotten about. List them below:

_____

_____

_____

_____

_____

_____

_____

_____

_____

_____

_____

_____

_____

_____

_____

_____

_____

_____

How have you confused God's incubation period with the enemy's assignment of delay?

_____

_____

_____

_____

_____

_____

_____

_____

What are you spiritually birthing right now that had been under attack?

_____

_____

_____

_____

_____

_____

_____

_____

CHAPTER 14

HIDDEN TREASURES

Father, I thank You that I have access to Your limitless Kingdom and every tool and resource inside it that will enable me to fulfill my destiny. I ask that You show me what my gift mix is, what my tools are, and help me use them effectively, in Jesus' name!

You are a potent and powerful tool in the Lord's hand. Don't forget that the Holy Spirit wants to help you discover your hidden treasure. Circle some of the hidden gifts incubating in your prophetic quiver:

Revelation

Disciple maker

Imparter

Equipper of the body

Repair and restore the Church

**Confront stagnant and stale
forms of religion that have no fruit**

Clear the path to greater unity

Creative or administrative gifts

Scribe

Songwriter

Author

Messenger

Calling the body to worship and prayer

Announcing a call to justice

Administrator of truth and justice

Knowing the times and seasons

Sensing the shifts in cycles and predicting when God is moving

The gift of foresight and vision

Warning and guiding the body

Exposing evil plots and plans so they can be foiled

Conductor of His power and glory

Transporting the Church out of the past and into the future

Transferring back the rights and ownership of stolen and usurped regions and places

Choose several of these hidden treasures and copy them below. How does God use them in your daily life?

_____

_____

_____

_____

_____

_____

_____

_____

_____

_____

_____

_____

_____

_____

_____

_____

_____

_____

_____

_____

How can you use them more?

_____

_____

_____

_____

_____

_____

_____

_____

_____

_____

_____

_____

_____

_____

_____

_____

_____

_____

CHAPTER 15

HEALING WOUNDS

Jesus, I give You my wounds. I don't want to live disabled by the things that have happened to me, and I don't want to operate in my calling with the potential to wound others or miss what You are saying. Today, I shake off the wounded mentality that has caused me so much shame and begin to step into my healing and hour of complete wholeness in Jesus' name!

What wound in me, if left unhealed, has the potential to wound others?

_____

_____

_____

_____

_____

_____

_____

A season involving woundedness can be preparation for major impact if we don't become bitter. What do you need to let go of now?

_____

_____

_____

_____

_____

_____

_____

_____

What causes a person to step out of the wilderness and still live like they are in it?

_____

_____

_____

_____

_____

_____

_____

_____

List three wounds or wounded mindsets that you struggle with shaking free from.

_____

_____

_____

_____

_____

_____

_____

Now list three verses/truths that, when ingested, will help you to heal and move on from these lies.

_____

_____

_____

_____

_____

_____

Circle the right answer—what matters most in your calling?

Stewarding your opportunities

Stewarding your heart

CHAPTER 16

LONE RANGERS

Thank You, Lord, that my family and tribe are coming and that there is a purpose in this crazy journey I have been on. Right now, I know You are connecting all the dots, and one day soon it will all make sense. I trust You that wherever I am going You are taking me from glory to glory and You will finish what You started, in Jesus' name.

Hi-ho, Silver, away! Honestly, Lord, sometimes I feel like The Lone Ranger because:

_____

_____

_____

_____

_____

_____

_____

_____

Write Psalm 68:6:

_____

_____

_____

Ask the Lord for a spiritual family:

_____

_____

_____

_____

_____

_____

_____

_____

_____

_____

_____

_____

Write the name of a person who might be a mentor to you.

_____

Is there someone whom you could take under your wing? You don't have to be mature, you just have to know a little more than they do. How can you be a friend today?

_____

_____

_____

_____

_____

_____

_____

_____

_____

CHAPTER 17

GOD APPROVAL

Holy Ghost, baptize me in the love of God that burns away my incessant need to be liked and approved. Take away my fear of being looked down on and give me courage to rise up and be who I was called to be no matter what people do or say about me, in Jesus' name.

On the Approval Addict Scale, circle where you rate.

1 2 3 4 5 6 7 8 9 10

When you are facing the fear of man, run into the secret place and get a second opinion! What does He say about you? If you don't hear anything, write down several verses that apply:

_____

_____

_____

_____

Pursuit of your destiny will take you through the season when those who are jealous will sell you out. Read Genesis 37:3-4.

Why did David's brother assassinate his character? (See 1 Samuel 17:28.)

_____

_____

_____

_____

_____

_____

_____

_____

_____

_____

_____

_____

_____

_____

_____

_____

_____

_____

Have you had seasons like this? How can you get past them?

_____

_____

_____

_____

_____

_____

_____

_____

_____

_____

_____

_____

_____

_____

_____

_____

_____

_____

_____

CHAPTER 18

MISTAKEN IDENTITY

Father, heal me of the orphan spirit and reveal who You are to me. Show me who I am and break off every label and lie that I have accepted in my life. I don't want to live looking through the lens of an outcast anymore, because I know You have called me into a role that requires knowledge of who I really am. Show me who I am, Lord, in Jesus' name.

Have you ever felt like a misfit in the Church? Has this affected you in a lasting way? Without knowing what you mean to the Father you will live your life constantly trying to prove yourself worthy of something you were already qualified for. Who are you anyway?

_____

_____

_____

_____

_____

Your key is the Father's perfect love, and it's time to encounter Him and use your key daily. How much time do you spend with the Father each day? How much time do you spend on social media each day?

_____

_____

_____

_____

_____

_____

_____

_____

_____

_____

_____

_____

_____

_____

_____

_____

_____

_____

Identity confusion and rejection can cause prophetic voices to live as outcasts. Paraphrase the story of Mephibosheth below. You can even put it in modern times and make yourself the main character! (See 2 Samuel 4:4 and 2 Samuel 9.)

_____

_____

_____

_____

_____

_____

_____

_____

_____

_____

_____

_____

_____

_____

_____

_____

In the space below write some of the labels either you or others have spoken over you.

_____

_____

_____

_____

_____

_____

_____

_____

_____

_____

_____

_____

_____

_____

_____

_____

_____

Now using a red pen, one at a time, cross them out as a prophetic act!

CHAPTER 19

FEARS EVICTION

Lord, heal me of Jezebel bites and narcissism wounds that I have been carrying—wounds that have kept me silent in a time I know You are asking me to rise up. I give You my voice and ask that You would awaken and revive what I let muzzle me and put it in a tomb, in Jesus' name.

FEAR'S EVICTION NOTICE

Fear, you no longer rule me!

I decree that (check all that apply):

_____ I will no longer be a generation that tolerates the silencing, the cancelling, or the assassination of the Church's voice.

_____ I will no longer edit/tame my voice in reaction to culture, the popular consensus, soulish opinions, or the worldly watchdogs.

_____ I will boldly speak up for those who can't.

_____ I will be a light in the darkest places others aren't willing to go.

_____ I will be part of the shifting of the tide of this hour and re-light the fires of this prophetic generation.

Get your behind out of your chair (Do it now! I'm not kidding around!) and stand in front of a mirror and read these out loud like you believe it!

How can you implement each of these?

_____

_____

_____

_____

_____

_____

_____

_____

_____

_____

I actually got out of my chair and went to a mirror (circle one).

YES   NO

CHATTER ATTACK

Lord, I rebuke the words that have come at me and the chatter sent to keep me in bed. Lord, I cancel and command them to be null and void and disarmed. Lord, give me discernment in this journey and help me not to fight people but the principalities and powers I face. Arm me and equip me for this in Jesus' name.

Write Ephesians 6:12 here:

_____

_____

_____

_____

_____

_____

_____

_____

Who does Ephesians 6:12 say your real enemy is?

_____

When satan shows up dressed in human skin, how should you handle him?

_____

_____

_____

_____

_____

_____

How can you separate the person he is using against you from satan's attack?

_____

_____

_____

_____

_____

_____

_____

Next time you feel a chatter attack, which of these will you implement?

_____ Rebuke the words

_____ Call a friend and gossip back

_____ Cancel the assignment

_____ Forgive the mouth it came from

_____ Stay in bed binge-watching *Gilmore Girls*

_____ Put worship on and get on with your day

_____ Take communion with a family member

_____ all of the above.

CHAPTER 21

FATHER WOUNDS

Father, baptize me in Your love and heal me of every father wound I have encountered in my journey. Today, I choose to forgive those who manipulated and controlled me, used me, and squashed me and my calling. Lord, I want to walk in honor, so please give me Your eyes to see people how You have created them to be, in Jesus' name!

What is step one to get free of your father wounds?

_____

_____

_____

_____

_____

_____

_____

_____

If you are ready, spend some time forgiving those who have hurt you in the past.

_____

_____

_____

_____

How can you cooperate with the Lord to forgive that person who is currently the thorn in your flesh?

_____

_____

_____

_____

_____

_____

_____

_____

_____

_____

_____

_____

Why would God require this before the next promotion?

_____

_____

_____

_____

_____

_____

_____

_____

Ask the Lord to help you to see people the way He sees them. (Try picturing everyone with a crown on their heads!)

_____

_____

_____

_____

_____

_____

_____

_____

If you have never done this, it may feel awkward at first, but write a letter below to the Father and ask Him to show you what He loves about you.

_____

_____

_____

_____

_____

_____

_____

_____

What did He say?

_____

_____

_____

_____

_____

_____

CHAPTER 22

BREAKING OUT

Lord, here I am. Here is my heart and my life. Use me. Have all of me. I am leaving the wilderness and this is the moment my whole life has been leading to, and I don't want it to pass me by. So here I am. Do what You want, in Jesus' name.

The sidelines are no longer my home because:

_____

_____

_____

_____

_____

_____

_____

_____

_____

_____

Send out an S.O.S. to the Lord in the form of Song of Solomon 8:5. Write the verse here:

_____

_____

_____

_____

_____

_____

Encouraging thought to chew on: In your journey through the wilderness, once you reach halfway, you're coming out!

How does the painful wilderness you have walked through equate with your anointing to break bondages and help set others free?

_____

_____

_____

_____

_____

_____

_____

_____

What would you say the number-one anointing upon your life is?

_____

_____

_____

_____

_____

_____

_____

_____

_____

_____

_____

_____

_____

_____

_____

_____

_____

_____

CHAPTER 23

THE FRESH WAVE

Father, thank You for making me this way. I see now how You haven't given me this call to alienate me but to use me powerfully to see the Church come back to what matters. I give my life to be part of this wave of change agents and reformers arriving on the scene, in Jesus' name.

Because of the way God made you, you wear peculiar glasses. What things do you see that others don't?

_____

_____

_____

_____

_____

_____

_____

_____

Draw your glasses here:

You are not the problem. You are an agent of change, something the earth is crying out for. What is it?

_____

_____

_____

_____

_____

_____

_____

_____

_____

_____

_____

_____

_____

_____

_____

_____

_____

_____

Ask the Holy Spirit to help you ride this wave and not miss what He has prepared you for:

_____

_____

_____

_____

_____

_____

_____

_____

_____

_____

_____

_____

_____

_____

_____

_____

_____

_____

_____

Draw your awesome, spiritual, Holy Spirit-propelled surfboard here:

CHAPTER 24

CHANGE AGENTS

Father, I am following You wherever You go. This is worship to me. It's my life of abandon to seek You and do what pleases Your heart. Lead me and I will go. Show me where You are going and what You are moving upon, and I will leave everything behind for it, for Your glory, in Jesus' name.

I know I'm different and I want to please God, not just to be a rebel for shock value like I did once when:

_____

_____

_____

_____

_____

_____

_____

_____

Reformation is reforming your corner of the earth to look like Heaven. What would that look like? How can you help?

_____

_____

_____

_____

_____

_____

_____

_____

_____

_____

_____

_____

_____

_____

_____

_____

_____

_____

_____

Why was Jesus the best reformer ever?

_____

_____

_____

_____

_____

_____

_____

_____

_____

_____

_____

_____

_____

_____

_____

_____

_____

_____

_____

_____

_____

If you got *your* hammer and tacked *your* 95 Theses on the Wittenberg door, what would it say?

CHAPTER 25

OIL CARRIERS

Lord, give me a love for people and even systems and institutions that often frustrate me. Give me such a heart for the areas I am called to reform so that I do it with Your heart and not out of a heart of disgust or judgment. Help me flow with Your healing oil in Jesus' name.

You want to be known for what you build more than what you correct. How can you avoid becoming a "Wreck-It Ralph"?

The wrong kind of reformation is the one that doesn't need Jesus at the center, and it comes with accusation against people and people groups instead of against demonic systems. List some examples. I'll start you out:

1. Dealing with social issues and injustices the wrong way—without the redeeming blood of Jesus.

2._____

_____

3._____

_____

4._____

_____

How can we love what we have been called to correct?

_____

_____

_____

_____

_____

_____

_____

_____

CHAPTER 26

COMMISSIONED

Lord, mantle me for this purpose. Commission me for a life of being sent into the places that need me most. Help me to be flexible and willing to go where You lead. I will take whatever post You send me to as long as You anoint me for it! In Jesus' name.

If I got to choose my destination I would pack my bags and hop on a plane to _____ _____ , but I think the Lord may be calling me to _____ _____ .

I can learn to be more flexible by doing the following:

_____

_____

_____

_____

_____

On a scale of 1 to 10 how confident are you that the Lord will equip you for the tasks He calls you to?

1 2 3 4 5 6 7 8 9 10

Read 2 Kings 2:9-14. Did God give Elisha what he needed to run his race? Today break the lie that He won't do the same for you.

_____

_____

_____

_____

_____

_____

_____

_____

_____

_____

_____

_____

_____

_____

_____

CHAPTER 27

BURNING MESSAGES

Holy Spirit, ignite my message and make it plain and clear. Show me that I'm called and commissioned to be a voice of change and help me walk boldly with courage and with the full permission of Heaven, in Jesus' name.

"Great moves of God are usually preceded by simple acts of obedience." —Steven Furtick

List ways that you have been faithful:

_____

_____

_____

_____

_____

_____

_____

Write Proverbs 18:16 here:

_____

_____

_____

_____

How does this verse relate to your message?

_____

_____

_____

_____

_____

_____

_____

_____

_____

_____

_____

_____

_____

_____

Are you willing to face barren years and ridicule to be God's mouthpiece on earth?

_____

_____

_____

_____

_____

_____

_____

_____

_____

_____

_____

_____

_____

_____

_____

_____

_____

_____

_____

_____

_____

Reformers have a tough gig. Study, then list some of the outrageous things Ezekiel had to do:

_____

_____

_____

_____

_____

_____

_____

What is your message? Are you beginning to see it clearer? Share what you feel like your message is below.

_____

_____

_____

_____

_____

_____

_____

CHAPTER 28

HISTORY MAKERS

Lord, I receive Your commissioning and let Your approval wash away the words that have been spoken over me and the insecurity and rejection I have lived in that said I could never be used. Today, I begin my odyssey in the Kingdom as a reformer for You, in Jesus' name.

Bill Johnson asked, "Why would anyone want to get up in the morning and not shape the course of world history?" This is not a rhetorical question! Write your response:

_____

_____

_____

_____

_____

_____

_____

Don't let the fear of man dictate your call. Stop holding back, stop hiding! I will take a step toward my destiny by doing:

_____

_____

_____

_____

List three things you can do to shift your mindset from victimhood to royalty:

_____

_____

_____

Write a "flipping the script" declaration over yourself that God is turning everything once used against you now to bless you!

_____

_____

_____

_____

_____

_____

CHAPTER 29

HEART OF A WARRIOR

Lord, I give You my future. I give You all my days on this earth and into eternity. I love to make Your name famous in the earth, to tell the world about You, and to tear down the kingdom of darkness in my wake. This is the moment of my second yes, to go where You send me and to do what You ask me to do, in Jesus' name.

When God asked me to do that strange, crazy thing it ended like this:

_____

_____

_____

_____

_____

_____

_____

_____

"You will have to fight...for everything you desire and everything you hold dear in this world. Despite what you feel, or what you may have been told, you have a warrior's heart, because you bear the image of God. And he will train you to become a great warrior, if you'll let him."
—John Eldridge

What is your response to John Eldridge's quote?

_____

_____

_____

_____

_____

_____

_____

The fields are ripe and ready for harvest (see John 4:35). Are you ready to go?

YES   NO

_____

_____

_____

_____

What does this mean: "For those who have said *yes*, you vote with your feet"?

_____

_____

_____

_____

_____

_____

_____

_____

_____

_____

_____

_____

_____

_____

_____

_____

_____

_____

_____

Draw three paths and label one "The Road Less Traveled." Why has God called you to that one? Do you see the purpose in it clearer now?

CHAPTER 30

SPIRIT OF ADOPTION

Father, use me to bring the world back to You and the Church who have forgotten you. Anoint me with the spirit of adoption and the love of the Father that cuts through to the heart and rescues the most broken and destitute. Help me live my life emptying orphanages and leading people into Your acceptance, in Jesus' name!

Write a prayer asking the Lord to break your heart with the things that break His:

_____

_____

_____

_____

_____

_____

_____

Q. How do you eat an elephant?

A. One bite at a time.

Q. How do you begin your ministry?

A. One bite at a time.

Where can you find one broken, destitute person or one orphan to start with?

_____

_____

_____

_____

_____

_____

How can you set the table for others in your life right now? Write down three practical ways you can show the love of God to people around you.

1. _____

_____

2. _____

_____

3. _____

_____

CHAPTER 31

FEET OF JESUS

Holy Spirit, take me back to the feet of Jesus and let me live my life camped there, fixed on You. Help me to always be teachable and moldable. Help me to stay a novice and never feel like I have seen it all or have arrived. Remove from me what isn't You and reinstate what I dropped or was cheated of by the enemy, in Jesus' name.

It's time you clear the slate and start again. It's time to pick up what you dropped in your season of warfare, opposition, and wilderness. Circle the relevant ones and spend some time journaling your prayers. It's time to pick up my:

hope and joy

tools and weapons of warfare

authority

new mantle (let go of the grave clothes)

unfulfilled promises

instrument (my pen, my assignment)

boldness and fire

Draw a picture of a jacket. This jacket represents your mantle (calling and authority). What does it look like? What has God given to you that is unique to you?

CHAPTER 32

SMASHED IDOLS

Lord, keep me set apart unto You. Increase my discernment so I can see the difference between You and the sly ways of the world. Keep me on fire and never let me get far from Your presence, in Jesus' name.

"An idol is something you have to check with before you say yes to God." How does this quote by Jack Taylor apply to your life?

_____

_____

_____

_____

_____

_____

_____

_____

_____

_____

The word *holiness* means "set apart." What purpose are you set apart for?

_____

_____

_____

_____

_____

_____

_____

The word *compromise* means a stance in between two different things. Why is God's Kingdom an all-or-nothing Kingdom?

_____

_____

_____

_____

_____

_____

_____

How can you tell the difference between the right thing and what looks like the right thing but isn't?

_____

_____

_____

_____

_____

_____

_____

What are some idols/compromises you have dealt with in your life?

_____

_____

_____

_____

_____

_____

_____

What are some idols and compromises you see in the Church right now?

_____

_____

_____

_____

_____

_____

_____

How do we get back to what matters again?

_____

_____

_____

_____

_____

_____

_____

CHAPTER 33

THE RIGHTEOUS ROAR

Lord, help me leave my cave and slam the door behind so I never go back. Help me to stand up for justice and not let religion shut down my righteous roar. Show me how to be a voice for this hour who speaks from Your heart and clears the airwaves of all the noise. I will be Your mouthpiece and Your messenger. Fill me with Your words, in Jesus' name!

Let the pure voices arise! I will be the new media, I will be the new sound, I will crash the airwaves with truth by doing the following:

_____

_____

_____

_____

_____

_____

_____

Write Proverbs 28:1:

_____

_____

_____

_____

Circle what your *righteous roar* in this hour looks like:

Refusing to hide

Being bold

Lifting my voice no matter the cost

Standing up for righteousness

**Being God's mouthpiece no
matter what the enemy says**

**Recognizing there is healing in
my words as well as truth**

Refusing to apologize for confronting lies

Being the new media

Standing up to censoring spirits

Not tolerating bullies and the Jezebel spirit

CHAPTER 34

THE PERMISSION

Lord, increase me! Expand me and grow me into all You have called me to be! Help me to grab my calling with both hands and occupy that space. Help me to be the heavyweight You called me to be and to be it unapologetically. I step into the 2.0 of this call upon my life, in Jesus' name!

It's time to step out of that place where you're just sitting on the fence waiting and hoping that someone is going to validate you. It's never going to come! I can unapologetically step into my calling because:

_____

_____

_____

_____

_____

_____

_____

_____

Write Matthew 11:12:

_____

_____

_____

_____

How does it apply to you?

_____

_____

_____

_____

_____

_____

_____

_____

_____

_____

_____

_____

What has God given you permission to do that man doesn't? Write it below.

_____

_____

_____

_____

_____

_____

_____

_____

_____

_____

_____

_____

_____

_____

_____

_____

_____

_____

Respond to the following: "The days of passive prophecy without power are over. Sugar-coated words are not going to take us anywhere." What does that mean to you?

_____

_____

_____

_____

_____

_____

_____

_____

_____

_____

_____

_____

_____

_____

_____

_____

_____

_____

CHAPTER 35

KEYS OF LEGACY

Set me on fire, Lord, and let me burn for You all the days of my life. Help me to step out into my movement, in this moment, in Jesus' name!

Write Zechariah 4:10:

_____

_____

_____

_____

What is this verse's lesson for you?

_____

_____

_____

Goliath's taunts pulled on David's destiny. What giants, who have been dominating and enforcing culture, have you aimed your slingshot at?

_____

_____

_____

_____

_____

_____

_____

God turns your mess into a message (see Rom. 8:28) and your message into a movement that is the mobilization of countless others whom God created to pioneer with you. What is that message summed up in a word or a sentence?

_____

_____

_____

_____

_____

_____

_____

When you look back on your life from Heaven's gates, what will you wish with all your heart *then* that you had done with your life *now*?

_____

_____

_____

_____

_____

_____

_____

_____

_____

_____

_____

_____

_____

_____

_____

_____

_____

_____

_____

_____

As a way to finish off your journal, draw a picture of a set of keys. This is your legacy. What is it? What are you leaving behind to future generations? Label each key.

ABOUT NATE JOHNSTON

Nate Johnston is a prophetic voice and worshiper who has a heart to see sons and daughters unleashed into passionate friendship with God and an effective supernatural lifestyle. Through his ministry school "Everyday Revivalists," he leads people from the basics of the gospel to being sent and released into their mission field, as well as championing and raising up emerging prophetic voices around the world. His burning cry and desire is to see the body of Christ become a beacon for the lost by raising up a generation that walk in the love and power of God, representing Him well. Nate and his wife Christy have three daughters, Charlotte, Sophie, and Ava, and live in Redding, California.

OTHER BOOKS BY NATE JOHNSTON

THE WILD ONES